THE
MORTGAGE
MAZE

Navigating Your Way
Through Real Estate Financing
in Today's Economy

Book and Cover design by Prominence Publishing. For information contact www.prominencepublishing.com

A special thank you to our Editor Anna Jackman.

Retail profits from this book are being donated the Project Hope Alliance in Orange County, California. For information, visit www.projecthopealliance.org.

ISBN: 978-0-9737453-7-5

First Edition: November 2016

CONTENTS

INTRODUCTION

Thank you for your interest in this book. We have gone to great lengths to source some of the top Mortgage Professionals from California. In fact, it took quite some time to find exactly the right people for this project. We are proud to let you know that the content you are about to read has even exceeded our own expectations when we first set out to publish this book.

The co-authors of this book were truly a delight to work with! And if you have the opportunity to be working with one of them, consider yourself fortunate.

INTRODUCTION

When it comes to real estate financing, consumers often have more questions than answers and it's difficult to know who to trust for the best advice. They may have friends or family members they can talk to, but it can be confusing when everywhere you look and everything you read seems to be giving your contradicting advice.

With so many different mortgage professionals out there, how do you choose? It is our hope that the information in this book will help make your decision a little easier.

In the chapters that follow, you will gain strategies, tips and highly valuable information from mortgage professionals from California. These professionals will provide you with the knowledge that you need so you can make decisions based on advice from their years of experience.

We are also pleased to share with you that Prominence Publishing is donating 100% of the retail royalites from this book to Project Hope Alliance. Project Hope Alliance is an Orange County nonprofit organization dedicated to ending the cycle of homelessness, one child at a time. They are doing amazing work!

If you are interested in helping or donating, please visit www.projecthopealliance.org.

To your success,
Suzanne Doyle-Ingram,
CEO
Prominence Publishing

ALTERNATIVE LENDING

Featuring Thomas Yoon

Thomas, tell me about your business and the types of customers you help

At Excelerate Capital, we are a full-service mortgage banking company, but really what we're known for within the industry is what we call non-QM loans. In the public sector, these loans are referred to as Alt-A loans and are also known as alternative loans. Alt-A lending is a scarce, yet much-needed service in our industry, which Excelerate Capital intends to provide to the masses by innovating new programs into the marketplace.

Can you tell us a bit about what led you to the field?

I actually stumbled into the industry in 2002 after I graduated from UCLA with a bachelor of science degree. Like most children of immigrants—my parents are Korean—I was led to believe that I needed to be a doctor or a lawyer, so I was actually planning to attend law school or get my advanced degree in business.

During that time, the subprime boom occurred in our industry. Many of my high school buddies were doing very well in the industry, and I started working at it during the summer months as a part-time job. I only intended this to be temporary. I got an intern-to hire management job at that time with one of the really big mortgage platforms. Out of 100's of applications 30 where selected into this program, only three individuals were chosen to join their team after a two-week training course. Being fresh out of college, I thought of myself as some kind of hotshot and brushed it off because I thought it would be easy. I didn't make the cut. I ranked 4th on the depth chart and the last person before the cut, this really affected my ego and my worldview at the time. I became discouraged. However, the funk dissipated, and immediately I decided that I wasn't going to allow a failure to define me, so I went all in on trying to set my feet in the industry, so I could prove to myself that I hadn't failed.

What drives your work? What's your passion?

I am a people person, and I enjoy the process of working in a group environment where things are always dynamic. I'm passionate about chasing goals in a team environment where the sum of the parts is greater than the individual. I love the journey, the process, the chase of the dream.

In terms of drive, it comes from my family background. I was a child of immigrant Korean parents, and I grew up seeing their struggle in the early years of my childhood. My parents worked seven days a week, from morning till night. I remember in my elementary years my father would leave work at 5:00 a.m., and I remember him always kissing me on the cheek and the smell of his cologne on my face. He would come home every night at 11:00 p.m. The only time I got to spend with him was on Sundays when he would allocate four hours to eating breakfast and going to church together as a family. The hard work and sacrifices my parents made for my sister and me to have a better life here in the States is a debt I can never repay. I learned at an early age nothing trumps hard work. You need to work exceedingly hard if you want to really succeed at anything. My drive is a product of my upbringing and early life experiences.

Thomas, let's talk about the variety of options for mortgages today. What is alternative lending?

Alternative lending essentially refers to loans and loan programs that don't fit the standard box that loan products exist in today. Lending guidelines became much more restrictive after the real estate bubble of 2008. Alt-A loan programs provide a bigger net for customers to qualify for mortgage financing. Alternative loans overlook the tighter, restrictive guidelines of today's loans. They're more "outside the box."

So how does alternative lending compare to regular lending?

There are certain criteria you possess that determine your eligibility for a loan: income, credit, and work history. The difference between alternative lending and regular lending is the documented evidence of those criteria. In today's rigid industry, with conventional or standard loans you would be required to provide two years' of tax returns, 1040s, and two years of W-2 forms. You may be disqualified because you may not have the right income verification or the perfect credit or the perfect work history. For example, many self-employed borrowers may find it difficult to fit inside those guidelines. With alternative lending, we can provide other ways to document and confirm your ability to qualify for a loan.

What's the biggest misconception that people have about alternative lending?

Most remember the 2008 bubble burst when the real estate market and our financial markets collapsed. As a result, everyone has a bad taste associated with what they call alternative loans, or non-QM loans. What we're doing with alternative lending now is vastly different from the loans of the past. The loans of the 2000s, which led to the housing crisis, were based on highly irresponsible lending.

With today's Alt-A loan, we are actually looking at the borrower's ability to repay. For example, we are analyzing FICO scores to determine a client's capability of paying his or her mortgage. Require a larger down payment amount than most standard loan programs.

Note: A FICO score is a person's credit score calculated with software from Fair Isaac Corporation (FICO) using the person's payment history, amounts owned, length of credit history, new credit, and credit mix.

For example, loan balances that exceed $625,000 in the greater metropolitan areas of the United States are considered jumbo loans. The jumbo guidelines are different from your standard agency products; those guidelines are even more restricted, so it's pretty much a tiny hole for everyone to fit into. Most people who went through the 2008 subprime bubble have credit blemishes, which means they currently wouldn't likely qualify for a jumbo loan. Those are the types of people we will look at and say, "That's common sense—they reestablished credit, they make great money, their FICOs are good, so they should be able to get a loan." They would not qualify under a standard jumbo loan, but they can qualify for an Alt-A loan.

So all the mechanisms of Alt-A loans in the past are nothing like those of the present. Despite the misconceptions, it is actually highly structured. There's a real and efficient process behind the ability to repay that debt or that mortgage.

What's the biggest pitfall concerning loans that people may not be aware of?

I believe the biggest pitfall is when people bite off more than they can chew. A great example I would use is this: Currently, newly constructed homes are booming all throughout southern and northern California. When you go to these model homes, you see a home at your price point, and you fall in love with the model home and all those bells and whistles, and the next thing you know, you're at the very high end of your qualifying ration. Now, on paper you qualify for that mortgage, but if you actually assessed your lifestyle, you would realize that you can't really afford that home. While paying back the loan, your lifestyle would have to change dramatically. You're used to potentially spending more on your leisure activities, your day-to-day lifestyle, or your vacations. Those things don't factor in when we actually do your prequalification.

Many people end up not looking at the total financial picture of their spending and instead only look at what they qualify for, so when they eventually move into their new home, they find themselves either strapped for cash or forced to make unwanted lifestyle changes.

How do you help your clients successfully qualify for alternative lending?

This happens naturally. A lot of it is just educating them about the options in alternative lending. Alternative lending, from its conception, was made to allow qualified borrowers to get access to money, or loans, that the current market does not allow. By educating and informing them about their options, more times than not, the conversion rate of borrowers or clients wanting to do the alternative loan is extremely high. So it's really about informing and empowering our customers to know all lending options.

It's about educating people on what Alt-A loans are, what these loans can mean to them, and how people can leverage their debt. Oftentimes, a large majority of our Alt-A loans are nonprime loans—people typically refinance out of them within a few years, so they're commonly temporary bridge loans. The need for these loans could be because of life circumstances or blemishes in credit that are explainable and sensible but prevented them from qualifying, or it could be a self-employed borrower who claimed a less-taxable income than what they actually make.

Alt-A loans are more of a need-basis loan, and are typically something that clients get into and then work actively with a mortgage professional to refinance back out of within the next three to five years.

Can you tell me about a memorable success story?

Today's Alt-A loan looks extremely different because the clientele base is typically high net-worth borrowers. They tend to have higher FICO score averages than your conventional standard clients because many of our government loans, like our FHA and VA loans, have a much lower credit grid.

One memorable client of mine was an extremely successful widowed business owner. She was a single mom who took over the business she shared with her husband. She worked in Newport Coast, and she wanted to buy a home in that area. She applied for a multimillion-dollar loan, and even though she possessed a 700-plus FICO score, made tons of money, and had millions of dollars in the bank, she still couldn't qualify for a loan with any of the major three institutions: Chase, Wells, and Bank of America.

She eventually heard about our company, Excelerate Capital, and was referred to me. I looked at all of her financials and told her within fifteen minutes, "Yes, I can do your loan. I'll close your loan in about two to three weeks." She thought I was kidding, but we ended up doing so, and I earned a client for life.

Essentially, the reason why she couldn't qualify for a loan was twofold: she was self-employed, and although the company revenue was millions of dollars, it had all these tax write-offs, and what it actually claimed as its taxable income was much less than what it really earned. The other issue was that she wanted to keep her current owner-occupied residence and rent it out because she was trying to move into a bigger home. Currently, as jumbo guidelines are constituted, you cannot vacate that home and have incoming projected rent. You need to already have that rented out and shown on your tax returns to offset the rental income or that mortgage.

With our alternative—Alt-A product base—we were able to work from her business and her personal bank statements and come up with an income. We did not use her tax returns, which she wasn't claiming enough income on, and then we were able to take her vacating owner-occupied property and use projected rental income to offset her debt.

These are two major components in standard financing that would have made it a failed deal automatically. She ended up being a perfect borrower for us. We funded that loan, which was a multimillion-dollar purchase loan, and we closed it in under two and a half weeks. She's now a happy client of ours and has referred us to all her friends and family. She was even happy with our rate, which was slightly higher than she would have received at the other institutions. For her, this was a need-based loan. She qualified for the loan, and now she's actively working with us to apply more income so she can refinance into a standard loan several years down the line. She has the ability to stay in the Alt-A loan or potentially refi out and get into a standard jumbo loan. She has all those options available to her.

This particular scenario is actually quite common. It's what we deal with on a daily basis with our Alt-A clients.

What would be your best piece of advice for someone who is considering alternative lending?

Do not listen to mass media about what alternative lending is. It's such a small percentage of the lending pie within our industry that there isn't enough education and information for people to really know about today's new Alt-A loans. I think the best thing to do is go to a licensed mortgage professional who actually understands the product base.

What is the first thing a person should do if he or she is ready to move forward? Should that individual contact a licensed mortgage professional?

Yes, a licensed mortgage professional who specializes in Alt-A loans. The main reason for that is because it's not a mainstream product. Even if the product base exists at a certain company, it may rarely utilize those products. So the loan officers, or the company itself, may not intimately know the programs. It's very much a niche product, so you would want to get involved with a company that really understands it and can educate the client on it and clearly explain the options.

What steps would they need to take?

It's pretty simple. You would want to have all your financial documents ready at hand, and you would want to give yourself a good initial consultation, of at least an hour to really get informed and know your options. Look around and make sure that you're working with a loan officer who really knows the product. It's that simple.

How could someone find out more about alternative lending?

He or she could contact me directly. My e-mail address is tyoon@exceleratecapital.com. I can also be contacted directly by phone at 949-220-4099.

About the Author

Thomas Yoon

Chief Production Officer
Excelerate Capital
17802 Skypark Circle, Ste. 100
Irvine, CA. 92614

(949) 220-4099 Direct
(949) 387-9980 Fax

http://exceleratecapital.com
Tyoon@ExcelerateCapital.com

Thomas Yoon has been in the mortgage industry for over 13 years. He is the Chief Production Officer for Excelerate Capital oversees production and operations for both Retail and Wholesale divisions throughout the United States. He inspires everyone on his team to obtain their goals and reach their full potential by providing leadership and direction. He has a proven track record of providing hands-on management and success in all activities requisite in the sales, sales management and operations of sales fields.

Awards and Recognition

- 2014 Presidents Club Member Top Manager at Banc Home Loans
- 2011, 2012 Top 5 producer at Pacific Mercantile Bank
- 2009 Outstanding Divisional Manager Award Catalyst Lending
- 2008 Top producing manager Catalyst Lending
- 2007,2008,2009 Top producer at Clarion Mortgage
- 2001 Military Leadership award UCLA
- 2002 B.A UCLA

FROM REAL ESTATE TO RESIDENTIAL MORTGAGE LENDER

Featuring Jackie Cuneo

Jackie, tell me about your business and the types of customers you help?

I'm a residential mortgage lender, so I work with clients who are looking to purchase or refinance properties including single family homes, condos, and 2-4 unit buildings. I work a huge spectrum of client types, from first time homebuyers to high net worth borrowers and business owners with very complex financial profiles.

I know that you have a background in real estate. How did you get into the real estate business?

I originally became licensed out of a desire to invest in California real estate myself. I owned a print broker business at the time, and decided that moving into Real Estate would allow me to draw on my experience as a business owner and enter an industry I truly love.

What was your time like as a Realtor?

Being a Realtor is probably one of the most challenging roles I've ever had. Many people have no idea how hard agents work for their clients, handling everything from high-level negotiations to property prep, to very small details like giving access to a painter or handing over a key. As a Realtor, I learned pretty quickly that having partners you can count on makes a world of difference in how well you're able to serve your clients and focus on building new business.

What made you consider moving into the lending side?

After a couple of years as a successful agent, I teamed up with another Realtor at my company. She brought huge charisma, the ability to build client rapport, and a wealth of sales experience to the table. I became the "nuts and bolts" gal—focusing with our clients on income analysis for our investor clients, working closely with our lender partners on preapprovals, and negotiating the fine points of our purchase contracts. I realized how much I like the mechanics of the transaction, and decided that moving into the mortgage side was where I could really focus on solving those complex problems and putting deals together.

Why do you think financing is so important?

Most clients finance more than half of their purchase, often up to 97% of the purchase price. From my point of view, they're purchasing money, and using that money to obtain a property. For that reason, choosing a financing structure that makes sense for the borrower, property type, and transaction can have an even larger effect on cost to own than the purchase price of the property.

Choosing a lending partner who can offer variety and guidance suited to your personal goals instead of just working with an order taker at a big bank can have a huge difference on your cost to own and long-term success as a property owner.

What are your guiding principles as a businessperson and lender?

I'm in this business for the long haul, both as a property owner and as a lender. I care deeply about helping my Realtor partners and clients succeed, by helping my Realtor partners learn how lending integrates with their business model, and by helping borrowers choose financing that will advance their long-term goals.

How did you decide what type of mortgage company to join?

There are 3 major types of mortgage lenders: retail banks, mortgage brokers, and direct mortgage lenders (sometimes referred to as mortgage banks).

Retail banks have a small suite of products and a single set of underwriting guidelines that work for some borrowers. Brokers are essentially matchmakers, but have little control over the loan process once the application is complete.

I choose to work at a direct mortgage lender, where we have several products to choose from, but where we process, underwrite and fund the loans in house. I can also broker loans when needed. This gives me a great blend of product variety, competitive rates, and internal control, so I can tailor financing for my clients based on their needs.

How do you help your Realtor partners and their clients?

Going back to my time as a Realtor, I know that the lender partner you choose to team up with can help or hurt you. A lender that overpromises or underperforms can cost Realtors real income, and put a client's initial deposit at stake—or worse— cost them the property. A good lender partner is a Realtor's advocate, educator, and technical resource to make sure that a purchase transaction goes smoothly, and that clients are happy with that agent from start to finish.

What do you see in the future for the real estate market and lending?

I'm sure we'll continue to see consolidation, but I do believe the direct mortgage lender model is here to stay as a great alternative to the "big banks". I also believe we'll see more nontraditional mortgage products, especially for investors who need specialty solutions for unique properties or nontraditional income sources.

What would be your best piece of advice for someone who is considering applying for a mortgage today?

Although it may seem like the money you're borrowing is just a commodity, the person who helps you obtain your financing can have a huge impact on your long-term cost to own and the success of your offer. As a borrower, find a lender who will work hard to find you the best financing structure for your individual goals, rather than just offering one or two options.

Consumers may not know that we're compensated based on loan amount, not rate, so we're just as motivated as they are to find the best rate and terms for them, but more importantly—to get the loan closed successfully.

One more thing: getting a mortgage these days is extremely documentation intensive. Make sure your lender is able to explain what is needed and why, and who will take the time to review any documentation you may not understand.

What's the first thing a person should do if they are ready to connect with a lender?

Make an appointment by phone or in person to discuss goals, and get the process started as early as possible. Success starts before the actual loan begins, with consultation, sometimes advice on how to improve credit, gather documentation, and to know exactly how much money will be needed to purchase.

If you're a Realtor looking for a mortgage partner, take the time to sit down with a lender in your local market to understand who's committed to helping your clients and someone who will help you to grow your own business.

How can someone find out more about working with you?

Visit my site at www.jackiecuneo.com to get in touch by phone, email, or connect via social media.

About the Author

Jackie Cuneo

Sr. Loan Officer
NMLS ID# 340022

C. (415) 948-5390
E. jackie@jackiecuneo.com
W. www.jackiecuneo.com

Jackie purchased her first home in San Francisco in 1997, and after more than a decade working in print manufacturing, became a full time Realtor in 2005. After 5 years as a busy agent/broker selling a variety of property types, she realized how critical mortgage financing was to clients' success, and transitioned into the lending side of the business. She takes a "big picture" approach to her clients' real estate goals, and designs effective mortgage strategies for her clients to obtain property and manage real estate debt.

Jackie has purchased, renovated and sold several properties and views mortgage financing as an integral part of a long-term wealth building strategy. She has built reciprocal referral relationships with Realtors, Financial Planners, Attorneys and other professionals to offer clients a true real estate success team when purchasing or structuring mortgage debt during critical life events.

Jackie is an avid gardener and has learned that long-term success requires a relentless pursuit of knowledge, planning, and the ability to quickly adapt to changing conditions. You can find her at jackiecuneo.com or connect on LinkedIn.

HOW TO QUALIFY FOR A MORTGAGE AFTER BANKRUPTCY

Featuring Melinna Rivera

Melinna, tell me about your business and the type of customers you help

I'm in lending, so I help people with their home finance needs. I help those who want to buy a house - those who want to move up or upgrade and buy a bigger home or people who want to move down, like retired folks or empty nesters who want to move into a smaller home. I also help people want to refinance their home and lower their mortgage payment or use their equity to buy an investment property.

Buying a home, whether it is a primary residence or an investment, is a very personal process and it is important for an individual to work with a professional that they can trust. Owning real estate is a visually tangible representation of personal wealth. The way one goes about financing such a significant purchase can be very taxing. I aim to make the whole process go as smoothly as possible. I help not just by facilitating the best loan product for my clients but by helping plan for a long term real estate investment strategy as well.

I see myself as a type of mortgage counselor who works with consumers and helps them make educated decisions about their home finance. It is always my goal to make sure people understand the process so they can feel confident about their decision. I know that there is a lot of information available online but I also understand that at times it can become overwhelming. That is what I am here for – to let people know the options they have to finance or refinance their home. Lending guidelines, procedures and policies are constantly changing.

It is my job to be up to date with current regulations and guidelines. I am constantly taking training and attending seminars to ensure that I know what is available and know what is best for my clients. I want to make sure that I can get the most favorable loan terms and all proper regulations are being followed throughout the transaction.

Also, I am originally from Tijuana and a native Spanish speaker and one of things I love to do is to help those people who are primarily Spanish speaking, because the information available to them is not always well translated, and as a result they are not always well informed about all their options. I am well equipped to explain things to them because Spanish is my first language.

One of the things that motivates me the most is that I am able to help the Hispanic community. Through my work history I've unfortunately have seen folks being taken advantage because English is not their first language. I really do not want people to get lost in translation. I want everyone to have a fair opportunity to home ownership.

What led you to this field?

This is more of a two part answer. There is the chain of events that lead me here and then the reasons why I decided to dive into it so deep.

I started in this field because when I graduated from college I took a job (that I thought would only be temporary) at a mortgage brokerage firm. I decided to get my license and originate loans because I saw the potential in it. All I wanted was to be in a position to make a living helping people and lending does that and it is great. I love what I do and look forward to helping people with their biggest purchase. I really never thought I would say that. It was awhile ago when I really did not see this industry in a flattering light due to my previous job.

Back in 2008, I worked as a legal assistant at a bankruptcy law office when we had the big recession. It was at a time when things got really bad with the subprime mortgage bubble. As a bankruptcy legal assistant, I helped people who got caught up in that mess. People who for one reason or another were facing financial hardship and needed an out. At that time discharging debt was a much needed relief for many. Most of us have heard or read about the horror stories of people losing their houses to foreclosure left and right and entire neighborhoods of foreclosed homes.

I was right in the middle of it and I saw the emotional toll that foreclosure does to a family. It was difficult to see so many families forced out of their homes. Filing bankruptcy was the only out for a lot of people during this time. Many who lost their homes still ended up with the debt of their second mortgage. Others just needed more time before their home was foreclosed and they had to move. For a long time I blamed the industry for putting people in such difficult situations. Some people lost their homes because of reasons that were out of their control, but sadly, some people also lost their homes because they did not have the right guidance. I also noticed that a significant number of the people who were losing their homes were native Spanish speakers. So that's why I want to help that community. Making sure people have the advice they need is one of the things that motivates me now.

I take a lot of pride in the work that I did while in the bankruptcy world. And the knowledge I gained only helps me have a clearer picture of people's finances. During my time working in the bankruptcy field I learned a great deal about how the credit system works and how unfair it can be and how easy it is to get lost without the right guidance. I do believe that there is a need for bankruptcy protection for consumers. I also believe that many issues can be avoided if one has the proper information and game plan.

My transition from bankruptcy to lending was kind of a transformative process. I associated so much of my identity with bankruptcy and the rhetoric of anti-debt. It was a real rewiring of my brain because I went from being the person who got people out of debt to the person who now gets people into debt.

As I mentioned, when I graduated from college I started a job at a mortgage company which I took out of curiosity. To be honest, for the longest time I didn't really care for real estate agents or loan officers, and I was curious to learn more about their jobs. There I met people who are honest working loan officers and real estate agents who actually care for people. These are people who survived the whole real estate bubble. I quickly learned the benefits of homeownership and how a mortgage is the cheapest way to borrow money. It was here where I saw firsthand that there is another way that I can help people achieve homeownership and I can give them the right advice on how to avoid getting into something that they don't really need.

Let's talk about how to qualify for a mortgage after bankruptcy. Is that common right now?

Yes, it is actually very common for people to have a bankruptcy in their credit history. I believe a record was set in 2008 for most bankruptcies filed in California and then 2009 and 2010 actually ended up breaking that record. I am surprised as to the stigma bankruptcy still has today. What I have found is that it is people are inscribing the stigma onto themselves. They wear it like a scarlet letter.

Often people fail to see that bankruptcy provides an opportunity to get it right the second time around. Depending on the lender and on the chapter of bankruptcy filed, one has to either wait 2 or 4 years to be able to qualify for a mortgage. This is more than enough time to rebuild one's credit. It does take a little planning but it becomes worth it at the end.

One thing that folks should keep in mind while rebuilding after a bankruptcy is to make sure that all the debt they had before is listed as discharged on their credit report. Unfortunately, collection agencies and credit monitoring sites are not always diligent about having accurate information of each individual. It is important for the consumers to find a way to track their credit as they are trying to rebuild it.

Things that we need to avoid having are items marked as "disputed" and/or "past due" on one's credit report after the bankruptcy is discharged. Those are the kinds of the things that I look at when I go and meet with clients. One thing that I do want to note is that bankruptcy does not impede one from buying a home. It is always a good idea to consult with someone that is equipped with the knowledge to develop a realistic plan.

When working with my clients, I make sure that everything is in order so they can move forward with their loan and I give them guidelines to follow so they have a better chance to qualify. Overall, banks will mostly be focusing on what's been happening in the last two years of their credit history, with the last 12 months holding the most weight.

What's the biggest misconception that people have about qualifying for a mortgage?

People think that bankruptcy is a life sentence and that there's no moving forward afterward. I often talk to people who don't even want to know what their credit score is. They just assume that it's bad and rather not know how bad it is. Because of this, people are shutting themselves down. People need to look at their credit score and be aware of it so they can plan ahead. If your end goal is homeownership, you need to know where you are right now and see if you could qualify now, and if not, plan the steps that are needed to take your credit to the appropriate place.

The thing about bankruptcy is that they always see it as it's almost a dirty word but it's actually a great opportunity to start again. It's a reset button that gives you the opportunity to learn from your mistakes, and plan for your future. Two years later you could be in your own home.

For chapter 7 bankruptcy, I recommend that they wait two years because they need that time to build their credit up again.

With some lenders we can even do a loan when a person is in a chapter 13. The difference is, with a chapter 7 you get rid of all your debts and then you're done; you get to discharge in about three to four months. But if you go to chapter 13 you go into a payment plan. There are programs available for people who have been in a chapter 13 for over 12 months. Making your payments on time to bankruptcy court helps a person re-establish their credit.

What's the biggest pitfall that people might not be aware of?

In my experience there are two major things that people tend to not think about. One is that often right after bankruptcy some collection agencies continue to report on a person's credit report. Two is the lack of trust in people in the industry.

People underestimate loan officers. Sometimes they

don't want to talk to a loan officer until they feel that they're totally "ready" but what they don't realize is that they can and should consult with a loan officer even before they're ready. This gives them a road map to get them to their home. You don't have to have things ready right now, you need to work with somebody that has a plan and can guide you as you go.

How do you help your clients successfully qualify for a mortgage?

I look at their income, credit and assets. I always talk to them to get a really clear understanding of how much they can afford. I want to be careful and give them the best advice for moving forward. So I try to get as much information as I can. I ask questions, such as:

- How much do you want to pay per month?
- How much can you afford as a down payment?
- Do we need to put you in a down payment assistance program?

Each case is different, but for the most part credit, income and assets are the main factors that I look at in each person's file.

Can you tell me a client success story?

Well there is one client that I've just helped to prequalify. His wife made him take the appointment with me. It was just him and he did not seem too motivated to buy a home. He had to file bankruptcy in 2012, and he was really concerned about that. Unfortunately, there is still so much unnecessary stigma associated with filing bankruptcy. I remember during the initial meeting with this particular client, when I started asking about his credit he had difficulty telling me about his bankruptcy. People are often so quick to self diagnose and automatically think they do not qualify. That is why it is always important to seek out and consult a professional. I reassured him, and let him know that it actually quite common to have a bankruptcy and that it does not mean that he automatically had bad credit. When I ran this client's credit we found out that he had excellent credit, even with the bankruptcy still on his record. So I was able to qualify him for a great loan program and a low interest rate.

When I told him this his body language changed and he was visibly excited to learn that home ownership was a very real possibility. That is what I really enjoy about this line of work; I am able to have a part in a family's ability to move forward in home ownership.

What would be your best piece of advice for someone who is considering applying for a mortgage after bankruptcy?

Plan ahead and consult a loan officer. It's important to know where you stand right now. If you're in bankruptcy, you actually have a clean slate. So try to plan how you want to work out fixing your credit, and rebuilding again. For a lot of people, what's helpful is starting with a secure credit card. That way, you can demonstrate that you are paying on time.

Also, always consult a professional. We are in a DIY era – everybody wants to do things themselves and they research everything online. Doing the research is really great, but there is no better experience than meeting with somebody who has lots of real life experience in the field. They will give you more accurate information about things like applying for a loan or what affects your credit most. You can't trust what you read online to necessarily be true.

What's the first thing a person should do if they are ready to apply?

Even if they're just thinking about it, consult somebody so you can get the guidance you need. For example, they may discover that they just need to make a particular payment or perhaps pay off some tax debt.

Another thing people don't think about is having a car payment. It doesn't necessarily affect their credit score, but it effects how much I can lend them. There are things like this that people need to keep in mind.

What I need to do an assessment is bank statements, retirement statements, taxes, and records of whatever other financial assets they have. When they come to me with this information, I can walk them through the steps they will need to take. Everybody has different things they will need to do. Especially with the Hispanic community, they don't look at credit the same way most Americans see credit. They have credit ratings, but they don't have the credit history. This is where talking with someone early on can really be to their benefit. For example, they may have cash. This is a big thing, having cash, but the bank doesn't like to look at cash, because they feel it could be money-laundering or something that's not legal. So cash is always really suspicious. So I counsel people to deposit the money into the bank and then wait two months. That makes the process a lot easier.

Do you know of any resources in particular that people can use to find out more about how to apply for a mortgage after bankruptcy?

I have a website with a lot of articles on building your credit. It's www.melinarivera.com. It's designed to give simple advice about the credit cycle, and building that up.

If you have any questions you can reach me directly, my number is 949-529-1341.

About the Author

Melinna Rivera

www.melinnarivera.com
Melinna.Rivera@gmail.com
Phone: (949) 529 1341

Facebook: RiveraMelinna
Instagram: MelinnaRivera
LinkedIn: Melinna Rivera

As a Mortgage Banker Melinna is focused in helping people achieve their financial and personal goals of becoming homeowners.

She started her career working in the legal field as a legal assistant at a bankruptcy law office. With care and dedication Melinna helped people who were facing devastating financial hardship have a new beginning. Having spent over five years in the legal field, she understands how diligent dedication will always result in the best outcome for her clients. Now she works helping people find the smartest path to homeownership. Her goal is to help her clients make smart financial decisions when it comes to purchasing a home.

Due to her unique experience she developed a keen understanding of how to analyse each person's individual financial situation and is able to find the best loan product for her clients. She has a thorough understanding of the relationship between credit and income and is able to provide the best service to potential borrowers.

Originally from Tijuana, Mexico, she moved to Irvine to attend University of California Irvine and graduated with a Bachelor's Degree in Gender & Sexuality Studies. She wrote her senior thesis as an analysis of the effects of undocumented student debt.

Balance is important to Melinna and when she is not working in facilitating the best loan possible for her clients, she trains for flexibility and she is a creative person at heart. Some of her hobbies include knitting, drawing and soap making.

WHAT DOES A LOAN OFFICER DO?

Featuring Sean McDowell

Can you tell me about your business and the type of customers that you help?

We focus on helping people that purchase homes. We have a lot of expertise around the steps involved, who the players are, and what goes into making a successful purchase transaction from the financing side. We also do refinancing, but refinancing is cyclical and typically based on rates while home purchases occur regardless of what interest rates are doing so we're typically focused on helping people buy real estate.

When someone comes to you, have they already picked out the house that they want to buy?

Preferably no. Financing the home is traditionally the biggest challenge in a real estate transaction. People often haven't investigated their own finances to ascertain what loan amount they can qualify for before going out shopping for a home, which is problematic. Good real estate agents have a quality loan partner to help their mutual clients determine how much they can afford. Real estate agents don't want to drive a prospect around to 15 houses only to find out they don't qualify for a loan.

It's important for anyone who is considering purchasing a new home in the next six to 12 months to talk to professionals like us first. We can help guide them in their preparations for qualifying for a loan. They might need to fix their credit, work on their down payment or they might need to pay down or restructure their debt. There are major factors involved in qualifying. Some people are ready to buy right off the bat, but 90% of people who come to us need to make some form of preparation. Once we complete the evaluation of their current financial situation, then we can pre-approve them so that our client has an idea of what loan amount and payment they can qualify for.

Knowing this gives them confidence, and when they do talk to a real estate agent, they know where they're at with regards to price point.

So you are really the first step for someone considering buying a house.

We think so. The majority of real estate transactions involve financing. It is prudent to investigate this first.

Do you have a particular type of customer that typically comes to see you or is it a big range?

It's a big range. We focus on everything from first time homebuyers who need a down payment assistance program, to people who can afford to put half down on an expensive property. We also see investors looking to flip properties or hold homes as rentals. Often these properties are in various stages of disrepair and require some creative options.

For lower income home buyers there are a lot of government assistance programs out there whether it be city, county or state. These programs allow people to buy homes with very little or no money down. There are many factors based on their current income range, their household size, the city or the actual census tract that they're considering moving into – there are a lot of variables that determine what they qualify for and how.

We're in Southern California, and here we have a fairly large population of non-American born families. One of the major deciding factors for financial stability and wealth in America is home ownership and the biggest hurdle to home ownership is typically the down payment. Some of our clients are new to the country or low income. They have trouble drumming up 20% of the purchase price, because in our area that can be a hundred thousand dollars or more. That said, just because people don't have the down payment doesn't mean they couldn't make the required monthly payments. They're likely already paying a comparable price in their monthly rent payments.

We can connect these clients with programs that will help. We provide access and education around programs that will help them get into a home with very low or minimal down payment. That allows them to start building their home equity and future family wealth.

On the other hand, we also have clients with multi-million dollar loans where they put half down and the down payment is a non-event. That's a pretty big range. We have everything from people in Long Beach, Santa Ana and Anaheim to Irvine and Newport Beach where people have fairly high dollar homes.

Can you tell me a bit about what led you to this career path?

I've been running successful teams since I was a teenager with a team of door-to-door salespeople selling local restaurant coupons. I was a top producer/manager in several fields prior to finding the mortgage business in early 2000. Success for me came while proving sales systems worked and then teaching others the techniques and scripts that worked for me. Coaching and mentoring are in my

DNA. Over my career I've studied countless gurus and taken a little bit from each one. Those experiences allow me to evaluate a person's current situation and help develop strategies that will propel them in the direction they want to go.

While there are people that consider "sales" a bad word, the fact of the matter is that any time you're attempting to get someone else to see something the way that you do or you're trying to change their mind, you're selling. In the financial world we are highly regulated. Compliance, product training and expertise are very important. However, once you have a base of knowledge the difference between those that are successful and those that struggle is the number of people that they can persuade to work with them. I've never felt that selling a product or service was overly difficult because it involves a lot of listening and providing solutions to real problems. Where it becomes difficult and why sales often has a bad reputation is because people try to "sell" an inappropriate solution to the problem that has been presented to them.

Let's talk about the variety of roles in the mortgage industry and what exactly the loan officer does.

Our position in the mortgage industry is that of a trusted advisor. A comparable trusted advisor in other aspects of your life would be your accountant, your CPA, your financial advisor, trust attorney, divorce attorney. Our clients see us as a trusted advisor when they have a specific issue, question or something that they need help with.

Mortgage loan officers and real estate agents don't always position themselves as the trusted advisor, even though they have the key to a lot of information that buyers and consumers need and want. One thing that's really important for us on the mortgage side is to become a source of relevant information that allows us to be in that trusted advisor circle. Another way of keeping that going is to have good solid relationships with quality financial planners, CPAs and attorneys.

We help our clients build their own internal network and the client becomes the nucleus of all of these referral partners. A first time home buyer may not know how it all works; for example, they don't know what the tax implications are going to be. So they need help. And they need to be referred to other professionals for things like home owners' insurance and so forth.

Our ability to build a support network for our clients makes us a valuable resource to our clients, because we have access to things that they didn't even know they needed before they came in to see us. It makes us trusted advisors in that respect, but it also makes us a referral partner for all the other types of businesses. Our relationships with professionals we refer our clients to are reciprocal as well and over time we build really, really strong businesses through that referral network, and long-term business relationships.

What's the biggest misconception people have about what you do?

The misconception is that all loan officers are the same. People may think that anybody could do what we do, however the range of advice that you get between what you find online and sitting down with an actual professional can be extremely varied.

Just like in any other industry, you have people that are average and you have people that are really good. The professionals in our industry that are really exceptional are of great value to their clients. They provide personalized advice that comes from a strong foundation of understanding in the industry. They will look at your entire financial picture and decide how a mortgage fits into your financial world.

How do help your clients successfully qualify for a mortgage?

Only by reviewing our clients' overall financial picture can we accurately suggest a course of action. The factors include, but are not limited to, the four C's: credit, capacity to repay, collateral (the property), and capital (down payment). It's so important to meet with your client early on in their process. It's not ideal to meet with someone who needs a home tomorrow because we would be limited in our abilities to help a client achieve that. Home buyers need to reach out early in their process and talk to somebody who can figure out how they qualify. There are no two transactions alike so tailoring each strategy to the situation is critical.

Can you tell me a client success story?

Many times people have come to me saying, "I don't have any money" or "I can't afford to buy a house." Over the course of eight to 12 months, we may suggest working with a consumer credit company on getting their debt get paid down and getting their credit score up. If necessary, we help them to establish a savings plan that they adhere to and we educate them about becoming a homeowner. So between all those pieces over the course of eight to twelve months, we can help them afford the down payment, qualify for the loan and obtain an interest rate that would help them afford the house. Through that mentoring and education, we are able to actually able to help them achieve their goal of home ownership – when they did not believe it was possible.

I can think of one client who originally came to see me in 2008. Even though the market has been up and down since then they made money selling their house and upgraded to a bigger home when they had children. What we do on the financing side is really just a vehicle to achieve what's really important: the family that occupies the home and their pride of ownership, stability and everything that goes with it. That is one example and they still keep in touch with me to this day.

Working as a Loan Officer

We have a 'customer for life' mentality. You have to have that if you're going to be in this business. Working in the mortgage industry is not something that you decide to do for a little while. If you're going to get into business you have to build a business. It's really, really hard in the beginning. If you're not prepared to put in the time and energy, then you should not get in it. Later on when people see your business they may think, "Oh they were an overnight success." Well, the truth is, it took five years to create that overnight success. You have to be willing to put in the time and energy and effort up front, and be a real, valuable person to others.

What would be your best piece of advice to someone who would like to launch their career as a loan officer further ahead?

1. The first thing is to DECIDE. Decide you want more out of your business and your

life.

2. Second, clear some time and create clear and concise goals. What do you want to accomplish? By when? What steps are needed to get there?

3. Third, create an accountability mechanism. Tell someone your goals and begin to chip away at the activities required to achieve them. DON'T let yourself off the hook. This is where the coach is critical. These are YOUR goals. Don't let you stop yourself from achieving them.

Call me. We can meet for coffee and discuss.

When you're looking for new loan officers to work with, what are you looking for? For example, where would they be in their professional career when they come to see you?

They would not be looking; they would be somewhat established already. They are professional loan officers who are on their way to being top producers. They have a desire to be a top producer. They want to progress their career and for whatever reason they feel like they're not currently getting the support they need to do that.

I'm looking to work with really self-motivated people. I'm not going to call you to wake you up in the morning. If you don't have a drive to succeed and you're just putting in time at work, then I'm not the right guy. But if you want to go somewhere, and you're working hard at it, but the things you're doing are not getting you where you want to go, then I'm possibly the coach for you.

The people I like to work with have their own goals in mind when we begin working together. I'm not going to re-invent people's goals for them. I discover what their goals are, and help them achieve those goals. I tell this to people all the time. It's important to me that I don't tell people what to do, because then they are doing it for me. For example, if someone wants to have a home buyer seminar, I will support that and help them with everything they need to do that, because they're passionate about the home buyer seminar. But if I come to him and say, "Hey you should really do a home buyer seminar." They're only doing it because I told them to do it and that does not help. If they're passionate about it, then I can help support them.

You provide support for highly motivated people who are already on track in their career, but need some extra support to get where they want to go.

We all need extra support. Nobody gets there by themselves. You think you'll do it on your own, but you just don't, because it's too easy to let yourself off the hook. If you don't tell somebody about it and have a mentor or other support to help you get there, you won't get there. I'm not saying it's not possible for someone, but it's so very, very rare that someone achieves their goals and doesn't credit some of their success to the support they have received along the way.

Can you tell me more about your style and passion as a business coach?

When I coach it's not about me, it's about my client. So whatever they're trying to accomplish, becomes what I'm trying to accomplish. When I wake up in the morning I'm thinking, "Okay Bill's got this, Joe's got that and Sally has this, so how do we accomplish those things?" It's really not about me, it's about whatever their goals are. That's what keeps me going, trying to help people hit their goals. I feel, "I'll get what I want, if they all get what they want." That's who I am, I want them to accomplish their goals. I get frustrated, more frustrated than they do, when they don't succeed, and I'm happier than they are when they do hit their goals. I don't take any of this lightly. It's very serious for me. There are people for whom this is a life changing opportunity financially. Money is not the most important thing at all, but the things that money will provide for these people, for their family – it can change everything. I have clients who send their kids to college with the money they make, and do things for their family that they weren't able to do before. Those are the things that change people's lives, and those are the things I think are important.

I've experienced this type of change first hand. The McDowell family tree is primarily loggers and farmers, that's my history. Working in the financial sector I'm doing something very different from what my family has done historically. I've seen what being successful in business can do for my family. It can be a big change for everybody in the family if you do it well.

About the Author

Sean McDowell

Email: sean@mcdowellfam.com
Tel: 714-697-8667

Sean McDowell was born and raised in a small town outside of Eugene, Oregon. He moved to California in 1999 and has been in the mortgage industry since 2000. He is also a licensed CA Real Estate Broker.

In addition to being a top producing loan officer, Sean's career also includes leadership roles at well-respected companies such as Impac Mortgage and Ameripath Mortgage as well as his current role at Prospect Mortgage. He has provided strategic direction and has overseen production at call centers with a focus on refinancing and retail branches servicing realtors and purchase loans. He has also managed entire divisions at publicly traded companies concentrating on mortgage loans, loan modifications, short sales and REO liquidation. Sean's well-rounded experience in addition to his extensive background in both sales and operations is widely recognized and proves to be extremely vital to fulfill the company's ambitious vision.

Sean is a proud husband and father of two amazing girls. Much of his "free time" is centered around family activities. Additionally, he enjoys playing golf, playing the piano and is a voracious reader.

Sean is active in his community working with many organizations including:

- Mortgage Bankers Association (MBA) Residential Loan Committee
- Orange County Association of Realtors (OCAR)
- National Association of Hispanic Real Estate Professionals (NAHREP)
- Rotary International
- Indian Princess (father/daughter group)
- Second Harvest Food Bank
- Ronald McDonald House

Project Hope Alliance

Each and every copy of this book sold on Amazon directly benefits Project Hope Alliance in Orange County, CA. We thank you for your purchase.

What is Project Hope Alliance?

There are more than 26,000 homeless children in Orange County. In fact, 70% of the homelsss in Orange County are families with children. Under the veil of affluence in Orange County, there are 26,000 children slpeeing in motels, shelters and couches. Children need a stable home in order to learn and thrive. Project Hope Alliance is working towards ending homeslessness for children in Orange County, one family at a time.

Please consider donating or getting involved with Project Hope Alliance. You can find more information at:

www.projecthopealliance.org

www.ingramcontent.com/pod-product-compliance
Lightning Source LLC
Chambersburg PA
CBHW070810210326
41520CB00011B/1900